Remembering the HIRAGANA

a complete course on how to teach yourself the Japanese syllabary in 3 hours

James W. Heisig

tered in any form without the written permission of the publisher.

Published by Japan Publications Trading Co., Ltd.

First printing: December, 1987

Published by JAPAN PUBLICATIONS TRADING CO., LTD., 1-2-1, Sarugaku-cho, Chiyoda-ku, Tokyo, 101 Japan

First printing: December 1987

Distributors:

UNITED STATES: *Kodansha America, Inc. through Farrar, Straus & Giroux, 19 Union Square West, New York, N.Y. 10003.*
CANADA: *Fitzhenry & Whiteside Ltd., 91 Granton Drive, Richmond Hill, Ontario L4B 2N5.*
BRITISH ISLES and EUROPEAN CONTINENT: *Premier Book Marketing Ltd., 1 Gower Street, London WC1E 6HA, England.*
AUSTRALIA and NEW ZEALAND: *Bookwise International, 54 Crittenden Road, Findon, South Australia 5023, Australia.*
THE FAR EAST and JAPAN: *Japan Publications Trading Co., Ltd., 1-2-1, Sarugaku-cho, Chiyoda-ku, Tokyo, 101 Japan*

10 9 8 7 6

ISBN 0-87040-765-1
ISBN (JAPAN) 4-88996-004-X

Printed in Japan

CONTENTS

Contents

INTRODUCTION

The *aim* of this little book is a modest one: to teach you how to write the Japanese *hiragana* from memory. The *promise* it makes is outlandish: to complete the task in three hours.

The book did not grow out of classroom experience and is not intended for classroom use. For one thing, I am not a language instructor. For another, all of my students are Japanese who knew the *hiragana* by first grade or before. I did not absorb myself in research on the Japanese syllabaries — surveying existing methods, drafting new mnemonic techniques, testing them out systematically on a group of students, carefully clocking the results — and only then deliver a completed manuscript to the publishers. But neither did the whole thing simply drop into my lap one day unexpectedly. The facts of the matter are a lot humbler: I wrote the book on a dare.

A visiting professor who had studied my earlier volumes on *Remembering the Kanji* was having trouble remembering the *hiragana* and casually tossed the challenge at my feet one evening over a mug of beer: "Why hasn't anybody figured out an easy way to learn the syllabary?" I didn't know if anyone had or not, but the next morning I took a sheet of white paper and wrote in large bold letters the title you see on the cover of this book. I set the paper on the corner of my desk and resolved not to write another line until I was satisfied I had grounds to justify its boast. From the very beginning, then, I was aware that I was up to something outlandish. Fortunately, the chore turned out to be a lot easier than I had anticipated, and the entire text was completed in a few days.

More important than how this book came to be written is

what it will do for you, and what it will not do. It *will* help you teach yourself the writing and reading of all 46 characters of the Japanese *hiragana* syllabary from memory in three hours or less. It *will not* teach you anything about the Chinese characters (*kanji*) or the other Japanese syllabary used mainly for foreign words, the *katakana*.

By three hours, I mean *three cumulative hours* of hard, solitary work on the *hiragana* themselves, not three continuous hours of unbroken study, and certainly not three hours in a classroom with a teacher and other students. You will be asked to take a break after each lesson. This is meant to increase your efficiency by helping you concentrate all your attention for short periods of 30 minutes or less. If you were to do two lessons a day, you would complete the six lessons on the third day. This strikes me as the ideal way to proceed. It will take you an additional 20 minutes or so to read through this Introduction, the comments at the beginning and end of each chapter, and the Postscript. You *could* skip this material, but I think you will find it worth your while not to do so. The use of the Alphabetic Index at the end will be explained later.

The *hiragana* themselves are arranged in their "dictionary order," not in the order in which you will learn them. Following the instructions on each page will send you skipping forwards and backwards as you make your way through each lesson. Eventually you will be shown how to remember the dictionary order.

If you have already learned a few of the *hiragana*, you might be tempted to chart your own course. Don't. You would be better advised not to use the book at all than to get yourself lost in a devilish labyrinth of your own devising. The method builds up step by step, and you will need the principles taught at the earlier stages to follow the directions given later. If you must, rush quickly through the pages, but rush *through* them, not *over* them.

Finally, you should note that the equivalents given for pronunciation are only *approximations*. Even though, compared with English, Japanese is a "sound-poor" language, this does not mean that all its sounds exist in pure form in English. In general English vowels are longer and muddier than Japanese vowels; English consonants are harsher and more plosive than Japanese consonants. The ability to recognize and reproduce the difference is an acquired skill that has nothing to do with the subject matter of these pages: how to link sounds to written forms and vice-versa.

It only remains for me to express my thanks to two persons who guided this book on its way to publication. The scissors-and-paste work in the layout was done by Ms. Sasabe Midori, whose faithful attention to detail has once more put me in her debt. And without the continued interest and support of Mr. Nakamura Toshihide of the Japan Publications Trading Company, this book would probably still be no more than empty words hovering over a mug of beer.

Nagoya, Japan   James W. Heisig
23 September 1987

⇢ Go to page 51

THE HIRAGANA

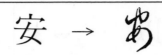 **a**

The first two strokes of the syllable *a*, as we just learned, form a **dagger**. (Its "blade" bends gently to the right in order to flow naturally into the next stroke). Below the **dagger** is the **no-parking sign** referred to earlier in passing.

(Note that when the *hiragana* for **no** is used as a "piece" of another *hiragana*, the cross-slash protrudes out the top slightly. Think of this protrusion as the post on which the **no-parking sign** is hanging.)

To put it all together, we need a word that suggests the vowel sound *a*. Let us take the playful little **otter**. See him swimming on his back in the middle of a pond whose banks are picketed on all sides by **no-parking signs**. On his tummy are a stack of **daggers** which he is tossing one by one at the signs, clapping his paws with glee each time he hits a bull's eye.

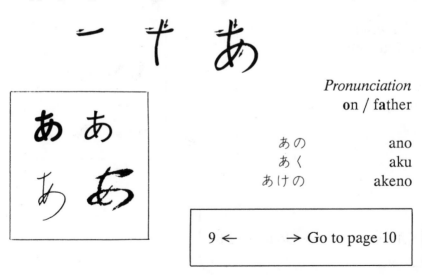

Pronunciation
on / father

あの	ano
あく	aku
あけの	akeno

9 ←   → Go to page 10

i

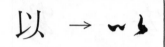

い

The roman letter **i** is drawn with two strokes, one main stroke and a dot to cap it off. So is the *hiragana* we are going to learn now. The first strokes of the two are almost identical. And just as, when you are writing quickly, the dot on your **i** often ends off over to the right, so is the second, shorter stroke of the *hiragana* always set to the right.

When you practice writing the form, take a pencil and trace over the strokes as they are given below. Almost immediately you should "feel" the flow from the first stroke to the second. After practicing the form once or twice on blocked paper, test yourself on the examples that follow below.

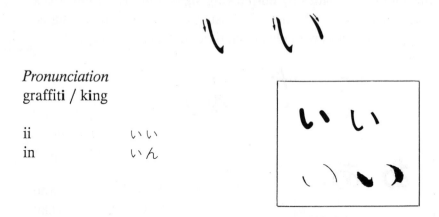

Pronunciation
graffiti / king

ii   いい
in   いん

46 ←   → Go to page 8

2

う   宇 → 宇   **u**

First the pieces. The short first stroke we will take to be a puppy's **tail**. Below that is the **2** (pronounced, remember, *tsu*).

As a word to identify this *hiragana*, let us take two cities (one German, one Italian) beginning with sounds very close to the vowel sound *u*: **Ulm & Udine.**

If you can remember to let *u* suggest those cities, it is a short hop to the pun that will help you remember this *hiragana*: a **tail** of **2** (*tsu*) cities.

Pronunciation
Ulm / Udine

うに	uni
うつ	utsu
にあう	niau

18 ←   → Go to page 17

3

e 　　　え

The pieces for the syllable *e* are a **tail, a chalk-line,** and the letter **n.** Let the sound suggest an **ape.** And what is our **ape** doing? He has drawn some **chalk-lines** on the floor of his cage to make boxes like the ones you are using to practice your *hiragana,* and is using a puppy's **tail** (attached to the puppy!) to practice brush-painting the *hiragana* ん.

Pronunciation
paint / neigh

en	えん
koeru	こえる
hae	はえ

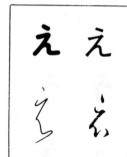

20 ←　　　→ Go to page 64

お 　　於 → 尤 　　**o**

This *hiragana* is not as difficult as it might look, once you isolate the elements that make it up, fix them clearly in an image, and then, keeping that image in mind, let the tip of your pen flow with the natural grace of its form.

The vowel *o* will suggest to us the figure of **Old Nick**, the devil himself. Unlike usual pictures of the devil, this **Old Nick** has not one but **2** (*tsu*) **tails**, each with a sharp **dagger** at the end. Note how he lashes them about menacingly.

Pronunciation
over / foe

おに 　　　　oni
おんな 　　　onna
おいけ 　　　oike

21 ←　　　→ Go to page 58

5

ka

加 → か   か

The *ka* of this *hiragana* provides the key word **car**. It is really made of two pieces, one familiar and one new. The puppy dog's **tail** drawn last you know. The part drawn before that is no more than a fancy sort of **dagger**, whose hilt is bent and lengthened, like the rounded handle of a **fencing sword**. So you might think of two **cars** (preferably two **cars** you know) decked out in all the appropriate gear and having a **fencing** contest. The **tail** belongs to a dog nipping away at the heels of one of the **cars**, as dogs are wont to do.

つ　カ　か

Pronunciation
In**ca** / **ca**lm

mannaka	まんなか
mukae	むかえ
Kannon	かんのん

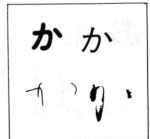

14 ←   → Go to page 32

6

The only real difference between the first three strokes of this *hiragana* and the **dagger** is the extra horizontal stroke. The reason is that they represent a long, heavy **sword**, which needs a sturdier hilt. Below it is the **hairpin** we just got through learning. The identifying word is, of course, a **key**. Putting it all together: a samurai is bringing his **sword** down (hence the slight angle at which it is drawn) on a **key** resting on a rock, to make a **hairpin** for his beloved. Be sure to pay attention to the great care and skill required for the feat, letting the image play freely for a minute or so in your mind.

Pronunciation
key / lucky

き り	kiri
い き	iki
あ き	aki

11 ← → Go to page 55

ku

久 → く   く

The shape of this next member of the *hiragana* family is formed exactly like the right side of the infamous computer-game mouth known as "Pacman" (**C**). If you think of the sound it makes munching up the dots on the screen as the **cooing** of a baby, you can actually see the word **coo** in the computer graphics: **C** ooooo. Whether you find it easier to think of the く as a squared off *C* or as the mouth of a baby Pacman gulping down little *o*'s, you shouldn't have any trouble at all associating this simple shape with its pronunciation.

Pronunciation
cook / coop

iku	い く
kun	く ん
kui	く い

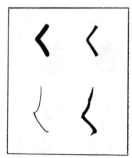

2 ←   → Go to page 29

け 　　　計 → 计 　　　**ke**

This *hiragana* is made up of two pieces. On the left, and drawn first, is a single slightly curved shape that looks like a **cape** that you might hang from the back of a stick-figure. (Draw one yourself and see.)

To the right is a two-stroke shape that resembles a **dagger** with the hilt at the top and the blade below.

The pronunciation of *ke* is close enough to the English word **cape** to get us going. Just twist the common phrase "cloak-and-dagger" into the image of a sinister figure in **cape-and-dagger** and the work is done. When you draw the pieces, think of them as images, saying the words to yourself as you go along.

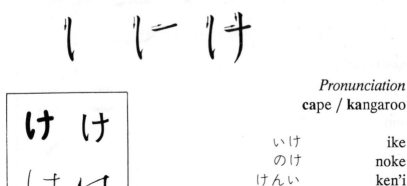

Pronunciation
cape / kangaroo

いけ	ike
のけ	noke
けんい	ken'i

25 ←　　　→ Go to page 1

ko

Try drawing a pair of rounded **combs**, the kind a woman might use to bind her hair into a bun. The first two strokes you no doubt begin with (the frame, without the teeth) form the very shape that give us our next *hiragana* — pronounced, conveniently enough, *ko*.

Notice the slight hooking at the end of the first stroke. It is absent in "cleaner," more modern stylizations of the *hiragana* and is not absolutely necessary. In any case, you will find that when you write the *hiragana* for *ko* the little hook forms itself rather naturally as you flow from the first stroke to the second.

Pronunciation
comb / ro**co**co

kono   この
kon   こん
keiko   けいこ

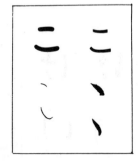

1 ←   → Go to page 22

10

さ

左 → さ

Beneath the familiar **dagger** is the lower half of the piece meaning **combs**. Let us call it a **hairpin** to remember the similarity of form. The key word here is a **sock**, a particularly old and raunchy one that some lady of questionable taste has stuck in her hair using a **dagger** as a **hairpin** to hold it in place.

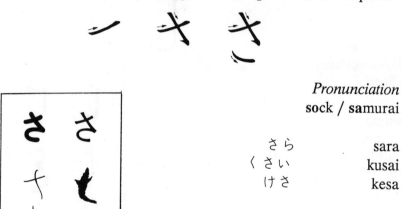

Pronunciation
sock / **samurai**

さら	sara
くさい	kusai
けさ	kesa

PS. Observe that the third stroke is joined to the second in typeset letters. The more you write this hiragana *(especially if you follow the model given above) and the faster you get, the more you will see how naturally the lines blend together.*

16 ←   → Go to page 7

11

shi

し

The shape of this *hiragana*—obviously a **fishhook**--is as easy to remember as its key word, **sheep**. To line the two together, picture yourself angling with a **sheep** dangling at the end of your **fishhook** instead of the customary worm.

じ

Pronunciation
sheep / pu**shy**

shima	しま
anshin	あんしん
sushi	すし

し　し
し　ミ

12

す

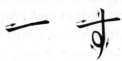

su

The key word from the syllable *su* will be **soup**. Attached to the **dagger** is a little curl which is in fact a single piece of **macaroni**. (Note how it differs from the **boomerang** by curling downwards and to the left.) All that remains is to imagine yourself at a posh restaurant stabbing **macaroni** noodles in your soup with a stiletto. Look! You've got one on the end of your **dagger!**

Pronunciation
soon / **suit**

りす	risu
すね	sune
すら	sura

24 ←   → Go to page 33

13

Se is for **seance**, a picture of which we will draw with the simple elements that make up his *hiragana*. First we have two **daggers**, drawn so that their hilts share a common, horizontal line. The last line, drawn on the bottom, is the familiar **chalk-line**.

Putting it all together: you draw a **chalk-line** circle on the ground and sit in the middle of it. With each hand you drive one of the **daggers** into the **chalk-line** and keep a hold of it, thus joining you to the magic circle within which the spirits will reveal themselves. Or some such hocus pocus. The **dagger** to the left is already in the ground; the one on the right is just about to be plunged in. As we have seen before, the second stroke naturally "hooks" up towards the third, though this is absent in more stylized forms of the *hiragana*.

Pronunciation
say / re**sale**

arimasen	ありません
setsu	せつ
sei	せい

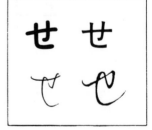

36 ←　　　　→ Go to page 6

14

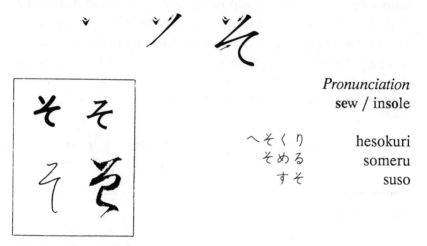

The pieces that make up the syllable *so* are a puppy dog's **tail**, a **walking cane**, and a letter **T**. Taking *sew* as our key word, you have only to picture yourself using a **walking cane** as a needle, threading it with a long **tail**, and *sewing* the monogram **T** on — what else — a **T**-shirt.

Pronunciation
sew / insole

へそくり	hesokuri
そめる	someru
すそ	suso

PS. In time, the first two strokes will naturally fuse, as in the typeset form at the top. The variable thickness of the lines there imitate the strokes of a brush — the thinner the line, the less pressure being applied. So even if the lines appear to fuse, in fact a distinction is maintained.

19 ←   → Go to page 37

ta

た

Before going to the next paragraph, see if you can recognize the pieces of this *hiragana* on your own. We learned them back in Lesson 1. . . .

That's right! On the left is the **dagger** and on the right the **comb**. The pronunciation should suggest the word **top** to you easily enough. Imagine a **top** delicately balanced and spinning around on the point of a **dagger** you are holding in your hand. As the **top** spins, it spits out rounded **combs** like the kind we first pictured when we learned the *hiragana* for *ko*. The more vividly you "see" yourself ducking the **combs** flying out, the easier this *hiragana* will be to remember.

一　†　†こ　たこ

Pronunciation
tatami / **top**

intai	いんたい
tako	たこ
tachi	たち

39 ←　　　→ Go to page 11

16

ち  **chi**

Let the identifying word here be **cheese**, probably the first word to come to your mind anyway and most convenient for making a good, clear image out of already familiar pieces: the **dagger** and **2**. All you need do is imagine yourself drawing out your razor-sharp **dagger** from its sheath and slicing yourself a piece of **cheese** with **2** (*tsu*) swift slashes, like some flashy culinary Zorro.

Pronunciation
cheetah / handker**chief**

つ ち	tsuchi
の ち	nochi
ち ん	chin

3 ← → Go to page 39

17

tsu

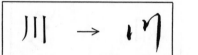 つ

In working foreign words into what is basically a sound-poor language, Japanese tries to get as close as it can. For example, the English word *two* ends up being pronounced *tsu*, the very *hiragana* we will learn now. Just our luck, the shape is exactly like an uncompleted Arabic numeral **2**.

つ

Pronunciation
tsunami / it's Ulm

kutsu	くつ
koitsu	こいつ
atsui	あつい

40 ←   → Go to page 3

18

て　　　　天 → て　　　　　　　**te**

Rather than a phonetic key word, we return to the procedure used at the very beginning, appealing to the alphabet—in this case, the letter *t*. Since you already have a pretty good "feel" by now for the way the *hiragana* forms flow when you write them, try drawing a capital **T** in two strokes, *hiragana* style, without lifting your pen off the paper. The form you will no doubt end up with is the one we are learning here.

Observe that the vowel we use to pronounce the alphabetic letter **T** in English is different from the vowel in the syllable we are learning here.

て

Pronunciation
tape / taint

よてぃ	yotei
てんきん	tenkin
さて	sate

35 ←　　　→ Go to page 15

19

to

と

Can you see the **walking stick** sticking out of the big **toe** in this form? Obviously the user is not very adept at walking with a cane yet! This *hiragana* should look like a doodle of someone jabbing a **walking stick** into his or her big **toe**. The only other thing you need to notice is that the **toe** points the opposite direction from the **finger** we met in the former *hiragana*.

Pronunciation
toast / **to**e

tokoton	とことん
hato	はと
toro	とろ

37 ←   → Go to page 4

20

な　　　| 奈 → 奈 |　　　**na**

Clear your mind of everything before you begin this page. It is important that you form a very vivid image to avoid confusion with the last *hiragana* we learned.

Let the sound *na* suggest a **door-knocker,** one of those grotesque gothic figures fixed to the middle of a great oak front door on a haunted house. See the little **tail** hanging on it? Give it a tug and **daggers** start flying out—a far cry from a welcome mat! But you take your distance and take aim with your trusty **boomerang,** throwing it again and again until you manage to break the ghastly contraption.

When you form your image and write the *hiragana,* you should try to follow the order of the pieces: **dagger** . . . **tail** . . . **boomerang.**

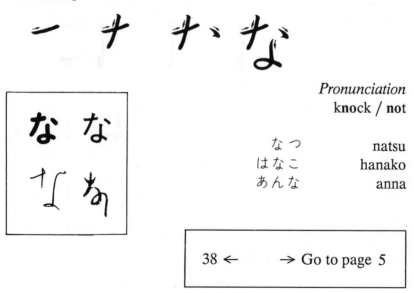

Pronunciation
knock / not

なつ	natsu
はなこ	hanako
あんな	anna

| 38 ← | → Go to page 5 |

ni

に

On the right side you see the *hiragana* we just learned for *ko*. But here the **combs** are out of the hair and glued firmly into your **knee-caps**, one on each side, so that when you put your legs together, the teeth of the **combs** interlock and you have a devil of a time getting them apart. Imagine pulling your **cape** around from the back and holding it between your legs to keep the **combs** apart.

Close your eyes for a few seconds and let the image take shape, focusing first on the **knee-caps** and then on its composite pieces, the **combs** and the **cloak**. Now open your eyes and look at the *hiragana*. You should be able to "see" the image before you. The next time you hear the sound *ni*, the whole ludicrous scene should come to life for you again.

Pronunciation
knee / anise

nin	にん
kuni	くに
niko	にこ

10 ←   → Go to page 53

ぬ　　　奴 → 奴　　　**nu**

This character will take about as long to learn as it takes you to read this short paragraph. The **maypole** has a **nude** statue spinning around on it, tossing **boomerangs** at passersby in the park. The **nude** supplies the key word for the syllable *nu*.

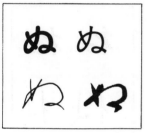

Pronunciation
nuclear / an**nu**ity

ぬま	numa
いぬ	inu
あけぬ	akenu

34 ←　　　→ Go to page 43

ne

 ね

Imagine being at a tedious academic convention where, to pass the time of day, you and a few colleagues have folded your **nametags** (the *ne* sound) into **boomerangs** and are waging war against a swarm of **wasps** gathered around a nest in the rafters.

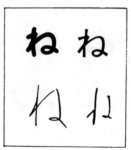

Pronunciation
nay / **ne**ighbor

ane	あね
yone	よね
netsu	ねつ

42 ←   → Go to page 13

 **no**

The internationally accepted sign for **no** is a circle with an angular slash running through it ⊘. The easiest way to draw it with a single stroke is to begin in the upper right, draw the slash, and then bring the circle around. The only other thing you have to remember is that there is **no** closing the circle.

When this *hiragana* appears as a part of another *hiragana*, with just the slightest alteration in shape, we will take it to mean a **no-parking sign**. An example follows later in this lesson.

Pronunciation
no / rhino

への	heno
のんの	nonno
くの	kuno

29 ←　　　→ Go to page 9

ha

波 → 

は

The key word for the sound *ha* will be the children's game of **hopscotch.** The first part of the character looks exactly like the **cape & dagger** we already met, so keep the same visual image you had there. The tiny loop at the end is a **boomerang**, shaped like this: . Notice carefully how it flows naturally from the end of the vertical stroke above it.

Instead of playing **hopscotch** with stones or bottle caps, imagine yourself using tiny **boomerangs** for tokens—and how difficult it is to get them to land on the squares because they keep looping back to you! As you draw the shape, say to yourself "**cape . . . dagger . . . boomerang,**" and the image and shape will fix themselves together in memory quite easily.

Pronunciation
shop / **ha**rlot

hanko	はんこ
hara	はら
haiku	はいく

は は
は は

57 ← → Go to page 30

ひ ‖ 比 → ひ ‖ **hi**

The key word for this *hiragana*, **heel**, is nothing more than the doodle of a pair of **handlebars** (drawn into that shape by putting two て s back-to-back). Instead of wearing spurs on the **heels** of one's boots, would it not be more fitting for modern men and women to wear little motorcycle **handlebars** that snap on the back of the heels just the way the spurs used to for the cowboys?

ひ

Pronunciation
heap / she

| ひ ひ |
| ひ ひ |

ひも	himo
ひいき	hiiki
ひまわり	himawari

65 ←   → Go to page 36

27

fu

The key word, **fool**, characterizes someone asked to show how many puppy **tails** there are. He answers **2** (*tsu*), because he doesn't notice the third one on top of his head.

Think of the piece for **2** as "flowing over" into the second **tail** so that you are not tempted to let it swoop downwards (as in the *hiragana* つ). The curves of the final two **tails** also flow naturally from the order of strokes.

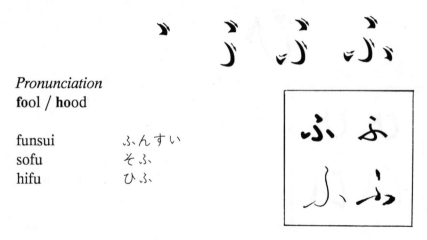

Pronunciation
fool / **ho**od

funsui	ふんすい
sofu	そふ
hifu	ひふ

PS. Resist the temptation to learn this hiragana *after the simpler model of the typeset character — even if that form seems closer to what you end up with when you write quickly.*

32 ←　　　→ Go to page 45

28

 **he**

Not forgetting what was said in the Introduction about the vowels generally being shorter in Japanese than they are in English, you can think of this next *hiragana* as a small **hay**stack, which it rather resembles and which happily also provides a link with the sound.

Pronunciation
hay / **sha**me

へん	hen
へい	hei
いへん	ihen

8 ←   → Go to page 25

29

ho

保 → 保

ほ

The key word **hoe** — a nearly perfect homonym for our next *hiragana* — is composed of **hopscotch** (which we just learned) with an extra horizontal line at the top. The added line represents in fact the **chalk-lines** on the **hopscotch** court.

Only the game is played slightly differently here. You stand with your two feet on a **hoe** and try to jump not *between* the **chalk-lines** but *on* them, hopping about as if on a pogo-stick, trying to land on the **chalk-lines** and kick up the white dust to prove it.

Pronunciation
hoe / **ho**ary

hori	ほり
hon	ほん
aho	あほ

26 ←   → Go to page 31

ま　　　　末 → ま　　　　**ma**

The key word is too simple for words: **mama**. The elements
that make it up are no less obvious. They combine the **sword**
and the **boomerang**. The image is not hard, provided you have
a distinct picture of **mama** in mind. **Mama** is standing in an
open field throwing large, heavy **swords** which are bent like
boomerangs so that they fly back to her. Watch her ducking to
avoid getting hit by the things as they whizz by.

Pronunciation
mama / motley

こま	koma
まつ	matsu
まんにん	mannin

30 ←　　　→ Go to page 38

31

The syllable *mi* easily enough suggests the word **meat** for an identifying key word. If you look closely at the shape of this *hiragana*, you will notice that it begins with the **7 dwarfs**, who are throwing **boomerangs** at kangaroos, and then carving them up for steaks with their dwarfish little **daggers**.

Pronunciation
me / en**em**y

minwa	みんわ
nakami	なかみ
nomimasu	のみます

6 ←   → Go to page 28

む 　　武 → 𛀞 　　**mu**

Our key word will be **moon**, the bright full **moon** glistening in the sky overhead—just the right time for a witch's brew. Under the **moon's** light, you are boiling a large kettle of **soup** into which you are tossing puppy **tails** and **hairpins**. You will have to let this image "stew" in your mind a while so that the **soup's** ingredients take on unforgettable qualities.

The first stroke of **soup** is shortened because it has to compete with other pieces for the available space. The curl at the end turns right, of course, because it has to blend into the piece for **hairpin**.

Pronunciation
moon / sa**mu**rai

むり	muri
むつ	mutsu
こむ	komu

13 ←　　　→ Go to page 61

33

me

The *hiragana* corresponding to the sound *me* has as its key word **maypole**. And a rather unusual **maypole** it is. Lacking one of their own, the neighborhood kids have stolen a **no-parking sign** and strung up a ball on it. To avoid getting in trouble for their prank, they have clasped an old **cape** around the **no-parking sign** to hide it.

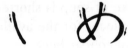

Pronunciation
may / inmate

tsume	つめ
ame	あめ
menko	めんこ

60 ←   → Go to page 23

 **mo**

Let the key word here be **mow**, and the image that of a mighty **sword** covered with hundreds of tiny **fishhooks**, which you are using to **mow** the weeds on the bottom of your pond — and catch yourself a few fish in the process.

Pronunciation
mow / remorse

きもの	kimono
もはん	mohan
もちいる	mochiiru

12 ←   → Go to page 19

35

ya

Let the key word for the syllable *ya* suggest to you your own back **yard** — more specifically a flower-bed or garden there. You are kneeling down on the ground, planting puppy-**tails** in the soil, pushing them down with your **walking stick** until they are all the same height, exactly one index **finger** long.

Note how the short vertical stroke we used in the *hiragana* for *yu* to begin the form for **finger** is left out here because it would overlap with the **walking stick**.

When you draw this character, rephrase the image verbally by putting the pieces in order: **finger** . . . **tail** . . . **walking stick**.

Pronunciation
yacht / cognac

yamato	や ま と
yakusa	や く さ
yahari	や は り

27 ←   → Go to page 14

ゆ

Think of the famous U. S. Army poster that reads "Uncle Sam Wants **YOU**" when you hear the syllable *yu*. Now focus on the finger pointing in your direction and note how the first stroke of this *hiragana* is a picture of an index finger (a little stubby, I admit) with the lead-in stroke representing the thumb. The final curved line you might think of as a **string** tied around the finger reminding Uncle Sam not to forget now that he wants **YOU**. Note how the **string** flows in naturally from the previous stroke, winding itself around the finger.

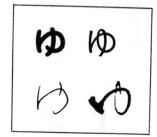

Pronunciation
cure / fury

あゆ	ayu
ゆらい	yurai
ゆき	yuki

15 ← → Go to page 20

37

yo

よ

The first English word that comes to my mind (and I hope to yours) when I hear the sound *yo* is **yolk**. The pieces we have to work with here are a puppy dog's **tail** and a very, very long **boomerang** (the full vertical stroke is part of it).

To fit these two pieces together, imagine a **boomerang** with one wing considerably longer than the other and a hole drilled in the middle. You stick the puppy dog's **tail** through this hole and tie a knot in it so that it doesn't slip out. You throw the whole contraption into the sky, while a group of people standing around throw egg-**yolks** at the hapless creature.

You can "read" the image like this to get the order of the strokes correct: people tossing **yolks** at puppies flying overhead, their **tails** knotted in long **boomerangs**.

Pronunciation
yolk / ma**yo**nnaise

yokei	よけい
yoko	よこ
yon	よん

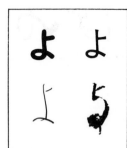

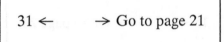

31 ←   → Go to page 21

ら  **ra**

The sound of this *hiragana* immediately suggests the cheer sound: **rah-rah-rah**. The only new piece is the short vertical stroke drawn second. We'll call it just what it looks like: a **1**.

Now all you have to do is imagine a mascot-puppy leading the cheers by wagging its **tail**, left and right, while the grandstands echo with the refrain: "**1-2** (*tsu*), **rah-rah-rah. 1-2** (*tsu*), **rah-rah-rah.**"

Pronunciation
rocker / rah

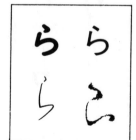

へら	hera
らん	ran
へつらう	hetsurau

17 ←   → Go to page 16

ri

利 → り

り

To begin with, let the sound *ri* suggest the figure of the **Grim Reaper,** the ominous **cloaked** figure with a long **sickle** slung over his shoulder. The **cloak** you already know. The long stroke to the right is the **sickle.** As you draw the *hiragana,* say to yourself: "See the **Grim Reaper** with his **cloak** and l-o-n-g **sickle.**"

Pronunciation
eerie / read

riku り く
heri へ り
nori の り

PS. The typeset form has the two strokes written together, whereas the practice model has them apart. Follow the latter. If you learn to write according to the typeset model, you will lack the proper "feel" for the natural flow of the hiragana *and eventually have trouble recognizing variations.*

54 ←   → Go to page 18

る 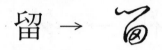 **ru**

The pieces here are simplicity itself: **row-row-row your boat** and **boomerang**. The syllable *ru* gives us **roof** as our key word. You rip the **roof** off a nearby doghouse, turn it upside down and, using a **boomerang** as your oar, **row-row-row your boat** ever so gently down the stream . . .

Pronunciation
rue / crew

はる	haru
さる	saru
ぬるい	nurui

43 ← → Go to page 44

41

re

礼 → 礼   れ

This *hiragana* suggests a **race**, albeit a rather odd one. Rather than competing to find a needle in a **hay**stack, the contestants are looking for the **7 dwarves** hiding in there. Watch the contestants as they come running out of the **hay**, prize in hand.

Note how the **haystack** naturally hunches upwards because of the lack of available space to stretch out.

Pronunciation
rail / c**rates**

hare	はれ
nureta	ぬれた
noren	のれん

44 ←   → Go to page 24

ろ  **ro**

Here we meet the longest key word in the book, for the shortest and simplest of images. If you have never had any trouble remembering that there are **3** *row*'s in "**Row-row-row your boat . . .**", you won't have any trouble here either, since the *hiragana* pronounced *ro* is written with a shape almost exactly the same as the numeral **3**.

ろ

Pronunciation
rotund / pet**ro**l

ろく	roku
いろ	iro
ろんこく	ronkoku

PS. I said "almost the same as the numeral 3." *To draw the form properly, you need the piece for* **7** *(to be learned in a later lesson) and that for* **2** *(tsu), which forms a bottom loop.*

23 ←   → Go to page 41

wa

The next three characters make use of a combination of two pieces, both of them new. The straight vertical line in the first stroke (which does not "bend" or "hook" to one side or the other like the **cape**) will be a **walking stick**. The figure *7* drawn next will stand for the **7 dwarfs.**

The syllabic sound *wa* suggests a **wasp**, which brings us to our image. As the unsuspecting **7 dwarfs** hi-ho hi-ho it through the forest and up a mountainside, leaning on their **walking sticks** as they go, a gigantic **wasp** sweeps down and picks **2** (*tsu*) of them up to carry off to its nest. The others start swinging their **walking canes** at the overgrown insect, beating it furiously until it lets go of their mates.

Pronunciation
wasp / I **wa**nna hold your hand

wani	わに
awa	あわ
wataru	わたる

41 ←   → Go to page 42

44

を 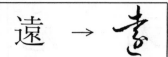 **WO**

The last of the *hiragana* (followed in the dictionary order by the very first one we learned) is in some ways the "cutest" of the lot. It might also look to be the most difficult, but — as you have surely learned by now — looks can be deceiving. The only strain, if you can call it that, will be to recall the key word: I'm **wo.k.**, you're **wo.k.** And the reason that we are both **wo.k.**, as the pop psychologists tell us, is that we treat one another with plenty of **T. L. C.** ("tender loving care").

Think of the form as a "branding iron" forged into the letters **T. L. C.** Begin by drawing a **t** (crossbar first), let it run into an **l** (slightly drooping downwards in the direction of the drawing), and cross it finally with a **c**. Fire the iron good and hot and then picture yourself branding someone you know with it!

This hiragana is only used as a particle and does not form part of other words in modern Japanese.

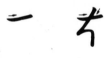

Pronunciation
how old / row over

28 ←   → Go to page 47

45

n  ん

The first of the *hiragana* forms we shall learn is also the easiest. It is exactly like the cursive form of the roman letter **n** (ん), except for the longer stem.

In romanized Japanese, whenever this *hiragana* is followed by a vowel, an apostrophe is added to avoid confusing it with *na, ni, nu, ne,* or *no.* We will see an example of the apostrophe later in this first lesson.

ん

Pronunciation
sing / kung-fu

52 ←   → Go to page 2

46

voiced mark

A **voiced mark,** as its name suggests, indicates that a consonant is to be pronounced with the vocal chords vibrating. Think of its two short lines ˵ as a doodle of the vocal chords.

When used with the *ka* row (namely, *ka, ki, ku, ke, ko*), the consonant is read *ga* (giving us *ga, gi, gu, ge, go*). Similarly *sa* becomes *za* (and so forth) *ta* becomes *da*, and *ha* becomes *ba*. You should be able to feel the voiced effect vibrating inside your throat. For all practical purposes the sounds じ and ぢ are both pronounced the same (*ji*), just as ず and づ are both pronounced *zu*. A number of examples are given below.

Pronunciation

zange	ざんげ	dobu	どぶ
zen	ぜん	giji	ぎじ
zoku	ぞく	gobi	ごび
mabo	まぼ	guzu	ぐず
debeso	でべそ	daba	だば
tsuzuku	つづく		

PS. These two short lines (drawn like straight quotation marks) are always inserted last, *after all the other strokes.*

45 ←   → Go to page 48

47

plosive mark

A **plosive mark** indicates a consonant that "explodes" on the lips with a "pop." Which is why it is shaped like a pop-bottle cap. There are only five of them, all from the same hiragana row. Thus *ha, hi, hu, he,* and *ho,* when inflected with the plosive mark, are pronounced *pa, pi, pu, pe,* and *po* respectively. Examples follow.

Pronunciation

kanpai	かんぱい
tenpura	てんぷら
senpu	せんぷ
inpei	いんぺい
pokari	ぽかり

47 ← → Go to page 66

48

THE LESSONS

LESSON 1

In this first lesson, you will learn 9 *hiragana* and will be exposed to nearly all the principles used throughout this course. Things might get a little more *difficult* as time goes on, but they will not get more *complex*.

Before beginning, open the book at random and take a moment to familiarize yourself with the layout of the *hiragana* pages.

* At the top of each page, on the inside margin and in large type, you will find a single *hiragana* character. On the outside margin in comparable bold type is its standard romanization (alphabetic pronunciation). This arrangement will aid you later in reviewing: by opening the book only halfway, you can flip through the pages at random so that only the alphabetic equivalents are visible and the *hiragana* is hidden from view.

* In the middle at the top is a box containing the Chinese character or *kanji* after which the *hiragana* form being treated derives. There is no need to learn it now, but when you are further along in your study of the *kanji* you may want to return to consult these frames.

* An explanation of how to remember the *hiragana* being treated follows. It ends with instructions on how to draw the form, stroke by stroke, following the standard of current textbooks used by Japanese children.

* Next, set against the outside margin, are a few English words (American pronunciation) to help you with the "reading" of the *hiragana*.

51

* Immediately below are a few practice examples, once again arranged so that you can block off the *hiragana* to test yourself. The examples are cumulative, using only those *hiragana* you have already learned. Do not skip these drills.

* Opposite the examples and set off in another box are a few of the variant styles in which you might meet the *hiragana*, two in print and two in calligraphy. Do not attempt to imitate them. They are given here for recognition only.

* Finally you will see instructions set in a small frame to the outside margin, reminding you where you have just come from and telling you where to go next.

At this point, if you haven't already done so, prepare several sheets of practice paper, boxes at least 1 cm. (½ in.) square. (You can find them at any stationery or kindergarten supply store.) This will help you keep the shape of your *hiragana* balanced much better than blank or simple lined paper will.

One more thing. Take a look at the clock and make a note of the time. In less than 30 minutes from now you will be asked to record the time you have spent on these first 9 *hiragana* in the box provided below.

→ Go to page 46

Time: Lesson 1

Congratulations! You have just learned 9 of the 46 *hiragana*, and probably spent less than 30 minutes doing so. On the opposite page at the bottom you will find a small box marked *Time: Lesson 1*. Record there how long it took you to complete this first lesson. From now on, do the same as you come to the end of each successive lesson.

A word about reviewing. If you take your time with each *hiragana* as you come to it, if you practice writing it several times, repeating the explanation to yourself as you go, and if you do all the drills on each page, there should be no need to retrace your steps. If you do get stuck, turn to the Alphabetic Index at the back, locate the problem *hiragana*, and go through the page all over again, from the beginning.

In case you are wondering whether learning to *write* the *hiragana* will also mean that you know how to *read* them, I can assure you that it will. Let me show you how easy it is. Try reading aloud the following six words:

いけん　　　のく
いんこ　　　あへん
くに　　　　この

All the sounds we have learned so far are contained in these words. Not to worry that you don't know what they mean yet — the only thing we are after here is learning the syllabary.

If you were planning on heading right into Lesson 2, change your plans and take a break now for at least 30 minutes. Go out for a walk or stretch out on the tatami. Your mind has been watching images fly around like shuttlecocks and should be a bit dizzy just now.

End of Lesson 1

53

LESSON 2

Now that you are refreshed, we are ready for Lesson 2. Just to flex your muscles a bit, write the *hiragana* for the following words:

iken	*noku*
inko	*ahen*
kuni	*kono*

The answers, if you didn't catch on, are on the backside of this page. Anyway, we know enough about what you do know; it is time we were back concentrating on what you do not know.

This lesson will take 8 *hiragana*, including some of those most easily mixed up by the beginner because of similarities in composition. As we shall see, careful attention to the pieces out of which they are constructed will spare you that problem.

Check your clock and let us be off . . .

→ Go to page 40

Time: Lesson 2

That's it for the 8 *hiragana* of Lesson 2. Record your time in the box on the previous page and get ready for another break. But first an added bonus for making it this far.

In the Introduction mention was made of the fact that the *hiragana* are laid out in this book in their "dictionary order." Since this is not the best order for learning them, you are having to hop around from place to place. Eventually you will have to memorize the dictionary order so that you can look words up quickly in an all-Japanese dictionary. To help, I am going to set the order to a little ditty that should make it just about as easy as it can get.

The first schooling most of us got with butchering French pronunciation came with a song called "Frère Jacques," the English rendition of which begins like this:

> *Are you sleeping,*
> *Are you sleeping,*
> *Brother John, Brother John?*
> . . . .

And you know the rest. Take the first line and change it to these four syllables:

$$A - KA - SA - TA$$

Just the first line for now. Let those four syllables resound inside your head for the rest of the day to the tune of "Frère Jacques" whenever you've got a spare moment. In later lessons we will learn the rest of the jingle and also find out what it all means. Right now you don't have enough *hiragana* under your belt to make the explanation stick.

End of Lesson 2

55

LESSON 3

Here we are over 1/3 of the way through the *hiragana* and you are probably well ahead of schedule. Just to make sure that you have the idea and aren't rushing ahead too quickly, let's take a minute to lay out the principles lying behind the learning you have been up to so far.

Actually, you have been led through a series of four stages which go something like this:

1. The roman pronunciation is associated either with its alphabetic equivalent or with a word closely related in sound.

2. This association—which we will call from now on the "key word"—involves an image which may relate either to the shape of an alphabetic letter or to a picture associated with the key word.

3. If the image is composed of pieces, those pieces are highlighted by focusing the imagination on them within the total picture.

4. The *hiragana* is drawn, repeating to yourself the "meaning" of the pieces as you go.

Everyone's mind works differently, but one thing is the same: even when your mental powers are running as efficiently as they can, your mind will occasionally trip over its own feet and trick you into thinking you know something that in fact you do not. The lessons have been kept short deliberately to minimize the effects of a loss of concentration. But even so, there may be particular *hiragana* you have trouble with. Have a look at them to see which of the four stages *your* mind tends to ride roughshod over. Then pay it more attention in the future.

There is no point to going over old territory, but just to make sure you have the idea, see if you can identify the key words (stage 1) for the following syllables:

i	*ni*
ke	*ku*
n	*a*

We will return to a check of the other stages in the course of later lessons, but try to think consciously of each of them as you proceed through the 6 *hiragana* of this lesson.

Well then, have a look at the clock, mark down the time, and let us be off . . .

→ Go to page 26

Time: Lesson 3

And so it goes with Lesson 3. Don't forget to record your time on the previous page.

No lesson will be as hard as this one has been. From here on, it's all downhill, so keep to your schedule and don't let up on your concentration. The lessons are short enough as it is, but you can't afford to get in too much of a rush and skip over any of the 4 stages we explained on the previous page.

And how have you been doing with our little ditty? Can you still recall the first line? You had better, because now it's time for a second line.

$$NA - HA - MA - YA$$

Try singing both lines, one after the other, until you have the melody, rhythm, and sound all together. Then just croon away at it during the day and once more before you fall asleep. In the morning you should find yourself waking up to it, and then we will be ready for the final line.

Meanwhile, it's time for another breather. If you decide you cannot stop yourself from reviewing, why not try opening the book just a crack to make the romanization visible, and test your knowledge of stage 1 for all the *hiragana* we already learned.

End of Lesson 3

LESSON 4

In the previous lesson we gave particular attention to the first stage of isolating the key word or phonetic equivalent of the *hiragana*. This stage is managed by mere word association, and every effort is made to insure that it goes effortlessly. In the 9 *hiragana* of this lesson we focus on the way we have been using the *image*, a slightly more difficult task.

The importance of a clear image cannot be stressed enough. If you have trouble, try verbalizing out loud what the image is, talking slowly enough that it has time to form in your mind's eye. If you take a moment to reconsider *hiragana* you had trouble with, you will probably find a nondescript image there. Associating it with particular memories of people, places, animals, and so forth — the first thing that comes to your mind is probably the best — will often help to get you going.

Even in the case of a *hiragana* whose explanation flows so smoothly that you don't see the need to isolate the stages, you should take at least a quick glance back over your shoulder before turning the page from one *hiragana* to the next and ask yourself, "What was the *image* of that last *hiragana*?"

If you have time now, you might even run through the *hiragana* you know to test it out. It shouldn't take more than a couple of minutes to flip through the book or use the Alphabetic Index at the back. If you are in a hurry to get on with Lesson 4, then at least take a moment to conjure up the image for the following syllables:

yo	*i*
ma	*ri*
na	*ho*
ta	*ni*

59

With that, we are back on our way again. Have a look at the time, and dig in your heels for what most people think are the most difficult of all the *hiragana*. You will be surprised how a little thoughtful organization on my part, and an extra moment spent fixing a clear and vivid mental image on yours, can help you breeze through them in no time at all.

→ Go to page 34

Time: Lesson 4

70% of the journey is over, and you have good reason to rejoice. Mark down your time on the previous page and take a good long break this time. You might even wait until tomorrow to do another lesson—just so you don't glide too far downhill through the remaining *hiragana* and forget to pay attention to *how* you are learning, which is almost as important as *what* you are learning.

To keep you company, here's the third line of the "Frère Jacques" ditty we have been learning:

RA — WA — N, RA — WA — N

Until later . . . .

End of Lesson 4

LESSON 5

The *hiragana* in this lesson are none of them very difficult, but they all require a clear mental image (stage 2 which we reviewed in the previous lesson). This time, let us concentrate on the role of stage 3:

> *Focus on those parts of the image that represent parts of the completed form.*

This sounds so simple that you might have been tempted to overlook it. But there is more than meets the eye.

When you form your first image, your mind will generally be ruled by mere *word association* with the image running on and off the set like a prop-man. The idea is to bring it to center stage, turn the limelight on it, and watch what it does when left to its own. You "coach" it along by focusing on the critical parts (the ones that stand for strokes), and then patiently wait, eyes closed, until the little magic lantern in your imagination starts spinning and something odd, ridiculous, disgusting, arousing, or otherwise memorable happens. Only then have words turned to image, and to an image you can trust as a mnemonics. This is the key step in the process you are learning here, so be sure and watch it at work.

In any case, why not try the following brief list, asking yourself what it was that made the image and its critical parts particularly memorable for you when you learned it:

ma	*mu*
ta	*yo*
su	*ki*

There is no need to worry that so many of the same pieces keep turning up again and again. This is done deliberately to

62

eliminate as much as possible the work of *brute memory* and let you concentrate on *imaginative memory* in the form just described. In other words, rather than clutter your memory with too many "pieces," I am asking you to flex your creative powers in building a large number of images out of a few simple ingredients.

Well, then, take note of the time and carry on with Lesson 5.

→ Go to page 12

Time: Lesson 5

If you followed my advice, you probably found this lesson something of a strain. But don't let up. There is only one more lesson, and it, too, demands the same attention.

By now you should know the entire "*Hiragana* Song." Let us just add a conventional ending so as not to leave the melody hanging:

A – KA – SA – TA
NA – HA – MA – YA
RA – WA – N, RA – WA – N
Now I know my kana! Now I know my kana!
Ding–dong–ding, ding–dong–ding.

It is time we cleared what this all means. The Japanese syllabary follows an order quite different from our typical Western alphabets. Think of the sounds as lined up in two directions. *Vertically* they follow the vowel sound present in all of the *hiragana* (except ん) in the following sequence: あ い う え お . I won't even bother to work up a mnemonic for that sequence; everyone I know learns it in a few seconds.

The second, horizontal order, is the one we just learned in our little song. Thus a dictionary will first list words beginning with あ , い , う , え , and お , and then pass on to words starting respectively with か , き , く , け , and こ . This sequence is followed by た , ち , つ . . . and so forth and so on. This is why it is important to master the order of the 11 syllables we learned in our little song. Without it, you will have to fumble around hit-and-miss in Japanese dictionaries.

Enough for now. Take a rest and gird yourself for the final lesson.

End of Lesson 5

64

LESSON 6

With this lesson you come to the end of your study, a mere 7 *hiragana* and two diacritical marks separating you from your goal of knowing how to write the Japanese syllabary.

I have deliberately left for this final lesson those *hiragana* that you might call "exceptions" in the sense that they entail slight distortions of familiar pieces. Meeting them here at this late stage, at least you can console yourself with the thought that there will not be any more of them.

→ Go to page 27

Time: Lesson 6

The course is run. Mark down your time on the previous page, and take a minute now to add up the time in all the boxes to find out how much time you spent learning the ひらがな. Someday you may want to encourage someone else to learn them and find it useful to have kept a record. The main thing, as you no doubt realized by now, is that being conscious of the clock helped you to break the task up into digestible pieces and give yourself encouragement along the way.

Total Time Spent in Learning the Hiragana

There are a few things you still need to learn about the ひらがな to use them to the full, all of them having to do with pronunciation: (1) the composition of diphthongs, (2) the transcription of lengthened vowels, and (3) the doubling of consonants. These are simple matters that you will find in the introductory pages of any Japanese grammar. There are no more written shapes to memorize. You are finished.

But even if you are confident that you have learned the ひらがな, you want to be sure that they *stay* learned — that they become a permanent habit, as "second nature" to you as the alphabet is.

To begin with, you should wipe out of your mind any hidden suspicions about this being impossible. If you have followed this little book faithfully, you are already well on your way to the same fluency that the Japanese themselves have.

Next, write the ひらがな as often as you can. Two things will happen the more you write. First, obviously, you will get faster at it and not have to stop to think about how individual

66

hiragana are constructed. Secondly, your writing will start to take on its own character, which can also mean some bad habits. When you feel this happening, it is best to seek the guidance of someone with a more cultivated hand who can point out what your writing lacks in grace and elegance.

My concluding advice, or rather sternest admonition, is therefore this: *Never again write so much as a single Japanese word with roman letters unless you are doing it for someone who does not read* ひらがな . Since you no longer belong to this group, you should have no more occasion to use roman letters for Japanese words than the average Japanese does. You might save yourself a few moments now and again if you jot down a note in the roman alphabet, but the inevitable cumulative effect of these apparently trivial "exceptions" is to forfeit the ability *already within your reach* to write with native fluency. Take the admonition to heart and I guarantee you will never regret it — not for a minute!

POSTSCRIPT

No doubt you are asking yourself now: if the hiragana can be learned so much more simply than I ever imagined, what about the かんじ ? Isn't there some way to organize them, too, so that I don't end up wasting a lot of time with too little to show for it in the end?

Yes, there is. And it can be done on basically the same principles used in this little book. Obviously there are a lot more of them and greater attention has to be given to procedure and learning techniques. I myself learned the かんじ this way and have written the results up in two volumes on *Remembering the Kanji*. Working from what you have learned here, you could as well do it yourself, but you will probably find that the books will save you a lot of time wasted in trial-and-error on technique and allow you to concentrate on learning the かんじ themselves.

It should be obvious to you if you look back over your shoulder at the course pursued in this volume, that this is not, and really *could never* be a method the Japanese might employ themselves. For one thing, the patterns of association and abstractions used often require at least an adolescent mind; for another, you already need to know the alphabet inside and out. For only slightly different reasons, the same holds true for the study of the かんじ . I have spelled this out in more detail in the volumes of *Remembering the Kanji*, but it all comes down to this: I can see no good reason why one *has to* learn the かんじ from someone who learned them as a child. Calligraphy, usage, etymology, and the like are another matter, of course, and for such things I am of the exact opposite opinion. But the work of

69

remembering how to write and pronounce the かんじ proficiently is not only slowed down but in most cases rendered impossible if done under the guidance of a Japanese teacher. The statistics bear this out with a scream; what I find it so hard to understand is why people keep blaming their own dull wits or lack of discipline, when the whole problem is with the method of instruction.

And finally, how about the かたかな , the sister syllabary of the ひらがな used mainly today for foreign loan words? Can they be learned much the same way I have just been following? To that question, I have no answer, only a proposal: try it. And if it works for you, and perhaps a few of your friends, write and let me know how you did it. I would be more than happy to review any such efforts, and if necessary endorse their publication.

POSTFACE TO THE 3RD PRINTING

The challenge with which the first edition of this book concluded — to produce a companion volume on learning the *katakana* — has since been met. Upon experimenting with the method outlined above for learning the *hiragana*, Helmut Morsbach, Reader in Social Psychology at Glasgow University, discovered that nearly all of the students were able to complete the task in less than three hours. With the assistance of Ms. Kurebayashi Kazue, he decided to take advantage of a stint as visiting professor in Tokyo's International Christian University to devise a similar method for speedy mastery of the *katakana*. After reviewing the first draft and learning of student response, I invited the two of them to Nagoya, where

70

we collaborated in producing a second draft, which was then sent out to volunteers for use and criticism. The final results were published under the title *Remembering the Katakana* (Tokyo: Japan Publications Trading Co., 1990). The volume includes a special supplement on "Learning How to Remember," which describes two methods for reviewing and refreshing memory.

ALPHABETIC
INDEX

あ ア	か カ	さ サ	た タ	な ナ	は ハ	ま マ	や ヤ	ら ラ	わ ワ	ん ン
い イ	き キ	し シ	ち チ	に ニ	ひ ヒ	み ミ		り リ		
う ウ	く ク	す ス	つ ツ	ぬ ヌ	ふ フ	む ム	ゆ ユ	る ル		
え エ	け ケ	せ セ	て テ	ね ネ	へ ヘ	め メ		れ レ		
お オ	こ コ	そ ソ	と ト	の ノ	ほ ホ	も モ	よ ヨ	ろ ロ	を ヲ	
が ガ	ざ ザ	だ ダ	ば バ	ぱ パ						
ぎ ギ	じ ジ	ぢ ヂ	び ビ	ぴ ピ						
ぐ グ	ず ズ	づ ヅ	ぶ ブ	ぷ プ						
げ ゲ	ぜ ゼ	で デ	べ ベ	ぺ ペ						
ご ゴ	ぞ ゾ	ど ド	ぼ ボ	ぽ ポ						